this book belongs to:

_____

WELL LOOK AT ME GETTING SHIT DONE

month:

TOP PRIORITIES / VITAL SHIT I MUST DO

- [ ] _____
- [ ] _____
- [ ] _____
- [ ] _____
- [ ] _____
- [ ] _____

IMPORTANT ASS DATES

BULLSHIT I SHOULD DO

- [ ] _____
- [ ] _____
- [ ] _____
- [ ] _____
- [ ] _____
- [ ] _____
- [ ] _____
- [ ] _____
- [ ] _____
- [ ] _____
- [ ] _____
- [ ] _____

SU	M	T	W	TH	F	S

WHERE THE FUCK IS MY MONEY GOING?

Personal Expense Tracker			
WRITE THAT SHIT DOWN!			
Date:	Description Of Expense:	Payment Type:	Amount:

ADD THAT SHIT UP: _____

WHERE THE FUCK IS MY MONEY GOING?

Personal Expense Tracker			
WRITE THAT SHIT DOWN!			
Date:	Description Of Expense:	Payment Type:	Amount:

ADD THAT SHIT UP: _____

ACCOMPLISHMENTS FOR THE MONTH, SUCK ASS FAILURES, GRATITUDE & OTHER

random shit

IMPORTANT SHIT I ACCOMPLISHED:

SHIT MY SORRY ASS DIDN'T GET DONE:

SHIT I WILL TRY HARDER TO DO NEXT MONTH(MAYBE):

A QUICK & EASY LIST OF SHIT I'M GRATEFUL FOR:

-
-
-

DOODLES & SHIT:

PEOPLE I WANT TO PUNCH:

-
-

OVERALL, THIS MONTH WAS:

O BASIC AS FUCK

O PRETTY AWESOME, ACTUALLY

O WHO CARES, I'M TIRED AF

O A SHIT SHOW, I PUNCHED SOMEONE

When life gives you lemons, freeze them and throw them at assholes who piss you off. It's time to give no fucks.

month:

TOP PRIORITIES / VITAL SHIT I MUST DO

- [ ] _____
- [ ] _____
- [ ] _____
- [ ] _____
- [ ] _____
- [ ] _____

IMPORTANT ASS DATES

BULLSHIT I SHOULD DO

- [ ] _____
- [ ] _____
- [ ] _____
- [ ] _____
- [ ] _____
- [ ] _____
- [ ] _____
- [ ] _____
- [ ] _____
- [ ] _____
- [ ] _____
- [ ] _____

SU	M	T	W	TH	F	S

WHERE THE FUCK IS MY MONEY GOING?

Personal Expense Tracker

WRITE THAT SHIT DOWN!

Date:	Description Of Expense:	Payment Type:	Amount:

ADD THAT SHIT UP: _____

WHERE THE FUCK IS MY MONEY GOING?

Personal Expense Tracker			
WRITE THAT SHIT DOWN!			
Date:	Description Of Expense:	Payment Type:	Amount:

ADD THAT SHIT UP: _____

ACCOMPLISHMENTS FOR THE MONTH, SUCK ASS FAILURES, GRATITUDE & OTHER

random shit

IMPORTANT SHIT I ACCOMPLISHED:

SHIT MY SORRY ASS DIDN'T GET DONE:

SHIT I WILL TRY HARDER TO DO NEXT MONTH(MAYBE):

A QUICK & EASY LIST OF SHIT I'M GRATEFUL FOR:

-
-
-

DOODLES & SHIT:

PEOPLE I WANT TO PUNCH:

-
-

OVERALL, THIS MONTH WAS:

O BASIC AS FUCK

O PRETTY AWESOME, ACTUALLY

O WHO CARES, I'M TIRED AF

O A SHIT SHOW, I PUNCHED SOMEONE

Never let someone treat you like regular glue.
You are sparkly ass glitter glue. Own that shit.

month:

TOP PRIORITIES / VITAL SHIT I MUST DO

- ☐ _____
- ☐ _____
- ☐ _____
- ☐ _____
- ☐ _____
- ☐ _____

IMPORTANT ASS DATES

BULLSHIT I SHOULD DO

- ☐ _____
- ☐ _____
- ☐ _____
- ☐ _____
- ☐ _____
- ☐ _____
- ☐ _____
- ☐ _____
- ☐ _____
- ☐ _____
- ☐ _____
- ☐ _____

SU	M	T	W	TH	F	S

WHERE THE FUCK IS MY MONEY GOING?

Personal Expense Tracker			
WRITE THAT SHIT DOWN!			
Date:	Description Of Expense:	Payment Type:	Amount:

ADD THAT SHIT UP: _____

WHERE THE FUCK IS MY MONEY GOING?

Personal Expense Tracker			
WRITE THAT SHIT DOWN!			
Date:	Description Of Expense:	Payment Type:	Amount:

ADD THAT SHIT UP: _____

ACCOMPLISHMENTS FOR THE MONTH, SUCK ASS FAILURES, GRATITUDE & OTHER
random shit

IMPORTANT SHIT I ACCOMPLISHED:

SHIT MY SORRY ASS DIDN'T GET DONE:

SHIT I WILL TRY HARDER TO DO NEXT MONTH(MAYBE):

A QUICK & EASY LIST OF SHIT I'M GRATEFUL FOR:

-
-
-

DOODLES & SHIT:

PEOPLE I WANT TO PUNCH:

-
-

OVERALL, THIS MONTH WAS:

O BASIC AS FUCK

O PRETTY AWESOME, ACTUALLY

O WHO CARES, I'M TIRED AF

O A SHIT SHOW, I PUNCHED SOMEONE

Start showing up like you know what the fuck you're doing. Wing that shit. YOU GOT THIS!

month:

TOP PRIORITIES / VITAL SHIT I MUST DO

- [ ] _____
- [ ] _____
- [ ] _____
- [ ] _____
- [ ] _____
- [ ] _____

IMPORTANT ASS DATES

BULLSHIT I SHOULD DO

- [ ] _____
- [ ] _____
- [ ] _____
- [ ] _____
- [ ] _____
- [ ] _____
- [ ] _____
- [ ] _____
- [ ] _____
- [ ] _____
- [ ] _____
- [ ] _____

SU	M	T	W	TH	F	S

WHERE THE FUCK IS MY MONEY GOING?

Personal Expense Tracker			
WRITE THAT SHIT DOWN!			
Date:	Description Of Expense:	Payment Type:	Amount:

ADD THAT SHIT UP: _____

Personal Expense Tracker

WRITE THAT SHIT DOWN!

Date:	Description Of Expense:	Payment Type:	Amount:

ADD THAT SHIT UP: _____

ACCOMPLISHMENTS FOR THE MONTH, SUCK ASS FAILURES, GRATITUDE & OTHER

random shit

IMPORTANT SHIT I ACCOMPLISHED:

SHIT MY SORRY ASS DIDN'T GET DONE:

SHIT I WILL TRY HARDER TO DO NEXT MONTH(MAYBE):

A QUICK & EASY LIST OF SHIT I'M GRATEFUL FOR:

-
-
-

DOODLES & SHIT:

PEOPLE I WANT TO PUNCH:

-
-

OVERALL, THIS MONTH WAS:

O BASIC AS FUCK

O PRETTY AWESOME, ACTUALLY

O WHO CARES, I'M TIRED AF

O A SHIT SHOW, I PUNCHED SOMEONE

Either you can or you can't. Either you will or you won't.
Stop fucking around and make up your mind.
YOU CAN AND YOU WILL. LET'S GO!

month:

TOP PRIORITIES / VITAL SHIT I MUST DO

- [ ] _____
- [ ] _____
- [ ] _____
- [ ] _____
- [ ] _____
- [ ] _____

IMPORTANT ASS DATES

BULLSHIT I SHOULD DO

- [ ] _____
- [ ] _____
- [ ] _____
- [ ] _____
- [ ] _____
- [ ] _____
- [ ] _____
- [ ] _____
- [ ] _____
- [ ] _____
- [ ] _____
- [ ] _____

SU	M	T	W	TH	F	S

WHERE THE FUCK IS MY MONEY GOING?

Personal Expense Tracker			
WRITE THAT SHIT DOWN!			
Date:	Description Of Expense:	Payment Type:	Amount:

ADD THAT SHIT UP: _____

WHERE THE FUCK IS MY MONEY GOING?

Personal Expense Tracker

WRITE THAT SHIT DOWN!

Date:	Description Of Expense:	Payment Type:	Amount:

ADD THAT SHIT UP: _____

ACCOMPLISHMENTS FOR THE MONTH, SUCK ASS FAILURES, GRATITUDE & OTHER

random shit

IMPORTANT SHIT I ACCOMPLISHED:

SHIT MY SORRY ASS DIDN'T GET DONE:

SHIT I WILL TRY HARDER TO DO NEXT MONTH(MAYBE):

A QUICK & EASY LIST OF SHIT I'M GRATEFUL FOR:

-
-
-

PEOPLE I WANT TO PUNCH:

-
-

OVERALL, THIS MONTH WAS:

O BASIC AS FUCK

O PRETTY AWESOME, ACTUALLY

O WHO CARES, I'M TIRED AF

O A SHIT SHOW, I PUNCHED SOMEONE

DOODLES & SHIT:

Life doesn't have to be sad as fuck.
Do more of what makes you happy.

month:

TOP PRIORITIES / VITAL SHIT I MUST DO

- [ ] _____
- [ ] _____
- [ ] _____
- [ ] _____
- [ ] _____
- [ ] _____

IMPORTANT ASS DATES

BULLSHIT I SHOULD DO

- [ ] _____
- [ ] _____
- [ ] _____
- [ ] _____
- [ ] _____
- [ ] _____
- [ ] _____
- [ ] _____
- [ ] _____
- [ ] _____
- [ ] _____
- [ ] _____

SU	M	T	W	TH	F	S

WHERE THE FUCK IS MY MONEY GOING?

Personal Expense Tracker			
WRITE THAT SHIT DOWN!			
Date:	Description Of Expense:	Payment Type:	Amount:

ADD THAT SHIT UP: _____

Personal Expense Tracker			
WRITE THAT SHIT DOWN!			
Date:	Description Of Expense:	Payment Type:	Amount:

ADD THAT SHIT UP: _____

ACCOMPLISHMENTS FOR THE MONTH,
SUCK ASS FAILURES, GRATITUDE & OTHER
random shit

IMPORTANT SHIT I ACCOMPLISHED:

SHIT MY SORRY ASS DIDN'T GET DONE:

SHIT I WILL TRY HARDER TO DO NEXT MONTH(MAYBE):

A QUICK & EASY LIST OF SHIT I'M GRATEFUL FOR:

-
-
-

DOODLES & SHIT:

PEOPLE I WANT TO PUNCH:

-
-

OVERALL, THIS MONTH WAS:

O BASIC AS FUCK

O PRETTY AWESOME, ACTUALLY

O WHO CARES, I'M TIRED AF

O A SHIT SHOW, I PUNCHED SOMEONE

Never be the prick who holds back laughter.
Live a little. Let that shit out!

month:

TOP PRIORITIES / VITAL SHIT I MUST DO

- [ ] _____
- [ ] _____
- [ ] _____
- [ ] _____
- [ ] _____
- [ ] _____

IMPORTANT ASS DATES

BULLSHIT I SHOULD DO

- [ ] _____
- [ ] _____
- [ ] _____
- [ ] _____
- [ ] _____
- [ ] _____
- [ ] _____
- [ ] _____
- [ ] _____
- [ ] _____
- [ ] _____
- [ ] _____

SU	M	T	W	TH	F	S

WHERE THE FUCK IS MY MONEY GOING?

Personal Expense Tracker			
WRITE THAT SHIT DOWN!			
Date:	Description Of Expense:	Payment Type:	Amount:

ADD THAT SHIT UP: _____

WHERE THE FUCK IS MY MONEY GOING?

Personal Expense Tracker			
WRITE THAT SHIT DOWN!			
Date:	Description Of Expense:	Payment Type:	Amount:

ADD THAT SHIT UP: _____

ACCOMPLISHMENTS FOR THE MONTH, SUCK ASS FAILURES, GRATITUDE & OTHER

random shit

IMPORTANT SHIT I ACCOMPLISHED:

SHIT MY SORRY ASS DIDN'T GET DONE:

SHIT I WILL TRY HARDER TO DO NEXT MONTH(MAYBE):

A QUICK & EASY LIST OF SHIT I'M GRATEFUL FOR:

-
-
-

DOODLES & SHIT:

PEOPLE I WANT TO PUNCH:

-
-

OVERALL, THIS MONTH WAS:

O BASIC AS FUCK

O PRETTY AWESOME, ACTUALLY

O WHO CARES, I'M TIRED AF

O A SHIT SHOW, I PUNCHED SOMEONE

A wise person once said "I fucking got this"
and kept fucking going.

month:

TOP PRIORITIES / VITAL SHIT I MUST DO

- [ ] _____
- [ ] _____
- [ ] _____
- [ ] _____
- [ ] _____
- [ ] _____

IMPORTANT ASS DATES

BULLSHIT I SHOULD DO

- [ ] _____
- [ ] _____
- [ ] _____
- [ ] _____
- [ ] _____
- [ ] _____
- [ ] _____
- [ ] _____
- [ ] _____
- [ ] _____
- [ ] _____
- [ ] _____

SU   M   T   W   TH   F   S

WHERE THE FUCK IS MY MONEY GOING?

Personal Expense Tracker			
WRITE THAT SHIT DOWN!			
Date:	Description Of Expense:	Payment Type:	Amount:

ADD THAT SHIT UP: _____

WHERE THE FUCK IS MY MONEY GOING?

Personal Expense Tracker			
WRITE THAT SHIT DOWN!			
Date:	Description Of Expense:	Payment Type:	Amount:

ADD THAT SHIT UP: _____

ACCOMPLISHMENTS FOR THE MONTH,
SUCK ASS FAILURES, GRATITUDE & OTHER
random shit

IMPORTANT SHIT I ACCOMPLISHED:

SHIT MY SORRY ASS DIDN'T GET DONE:

SHIT I WILL TRY HARDER TO DO NEXT MONTH(MAYBE):

A QUICK & EASY LIST OF SHIT I'M GRATEFUL FOR:

-
-
-

DOODLES & SHIT:

PEOPLE I WANT TO PUNCH:

-
-

OVERALL, THIS MONTH WAS:

O BASIC AS FUCK

O PRETTY AWESOME, ACTUALLY

O WHO CARES, I'M TIRED AF

O A SHIT SHOW, I PUNCHED SOMEONE

Chin up, dammit. Don't let your crown slip!

month:

TOP PRIORITIES / VITAL SHIT I MUST DO

- [ ] _____
- [ ] _____
- [ ] _____
- [ ] _____
- [ ] _____
- [ ] _____

IMPORTANT ASS DATES

BULLSHIT I SHOULD DO

- [ ] _____
- [ ] _____
- [ ] _____
- [ ] _____
- [ ] _____
- [ ] _____
- [ ] _____
- [ ] _____
- [ ] _____
- [ ] _____
- [ ] _____
- [ ] _____

SU	M	T	W	TH	F	S

WHERE THE FUCK IS MY MONEY GOING?

Personal Expense Tracker

WRITE THAT SHIT DOWN!

Date:	Description Of Expense:	Payment Type:	Amount:

ADD THAT SHIT UP: _____

WHERE THE FUCK IS MY MONEY GOING?

Personal Expense Tracker			
WRITE THAT SHIT DOWN!			
Date:	Description Of Expense:	Payment Type:	Amount:

ADD THAT SHIT UP: _____

ACCOMPLISHMENTS FOR THE MONTH, SUCK ASS FAILURES, GRATITUDE & OTHER

random shit

IMPORTANT SHIT I ACCOMPLISHED:

SHIT MY SORRY ASS DIDN'T GET DONE:

SHIT I WILL TRY HARDER TO DO NEXT MONTH(MAYBE):

A QUICK & EASY LIST OF SHIT I'M GRATEFUL FOR:

-
-
-

DOODLES & SHIT:

PEOPLE I WANT TO PUNCH:

-
-

OVERALL, THIS MONTH WAS:

O BASIC AS FUCK

O PRETTY AWESOME, ACTUALLY

O WHO CARES, I'M TIRED AF

O A SHIT SHOW, I PUNCHED SOMEONE

Okay fine, some pretty shitty things happened.
But forward is forward. LET THAT SHIT GO!

month:

TOP PRIORITIES / VITAL SHIT I MUST DO

- [ ] _____
- [ ] _____
- [ ] _____
- [ ] _____
- [ ] _____
- [ ] _____

IMPORTANT ASS DATES

BULLSHIT I SHOULD DO

- [ ] _____
- [ ] _____
- [ ] _____
- [ ] _____
- [ ] _____
- [ ] _____
- [ ] _____
- [ ] _____
- [ ] _____
- [ ] _____
- [ ] _____
- [ ] _____

SU   M   T   W   TH   F   S

WHERE THE FUCK IS MY MONEY GOING?

Personal Expense Tracker			
WRITE THAT SHIT DOWN!			
Date:	Description Of Expense:	Payment Type:	Amount:

ADD THAT SHIT UP: _____

WHERE THE FUCK IS MY MONEY GOING?

Personal Expense Tracker

WRITE THAT SHIT DOWN!

Date:	Description Of Expense:	Payment Type:	Amount:

ADD THAT SHIT UP: _____

random shit

IMPORTANT SHIT I ACCOMPLISHED:

SHIT MY SORRY ASS DIDN'T GET DONE:

SHIT I WILL TRY HARDER TO DO NEXT MONTH(MAYBE):

A QUICK & EASY LIST OF SHIT I'M GRATEFUL FOR:

-
-
-

DOODLES & SHIT:

PEOPLE I WANT TO PUNCH:

-
-

OVERALL, THIS MONTH WAS:

O BASIC AS FUCK

O PRETTY AWESOME, ACTUALLY

O WHO CARES, I'M TIRED AF

O A SHIT SHOW, I PUNCHED SOMEONE

Today is a good ass day to have a good ass day.
After all, you're a fucking champion.

month:

TOP PRIORITIES / VITAL SHIT I MUST DO

- [ ] _____
- [ ] _____
- [ ] _____
- [ ] _____
- [ ] _____
- [ ] _____

IMPORTANT ASS DATES

BULLSHIT I SHOULD DO

- [ ] _____
- [ ] _____
- [ ] _____
- [ ] _____
- [ ] _____
- [ ] _____
- [ ] _____
- [ ] _____
- [ ] _____
- [ ] _____
- [ ] _____
- [ ] _____

SU	M	T	W	TH	F	S

WHERE THE FUCK IS MY MONEY GOING?

Personal Expense Tracker

WRITE THAT SHIT DOWN!

Date:	Description Of Expense:	Payment Type:	Amount:

ADD THAT SHIT UP: _____

WHERE THE FUCK IS MY MONEY GOING?

Personal Expense Tracker

WRITE THAT SHIT DOWN!

Date:	Description Of Expense:	Payment Type:	Amount:

ADD THAT SHIT UP: _____

random shit

IMPORTANT SHIT I ACCOMPLISHED:

SHIT MY SORRY ASS DIDN'T GET DONE:

SHIT I WILL TRY HARDER TO DO NEXT MONTH(MAYBE):

A QUICK & EASY LIST OF SHIT I'M GRATEFUL FOR:

-
-
-

DOODLES & SHIT:

PEOPLE I WANT TO PUNCH:

-
-

OVERALL, THIS MONTH WAS:

O BASIC AS FUCK

O PRETTY AWESOME, ACTUALLY

O WHO CARES, I'M TIRED AF

O A SHIT SHOW, I PUNCHED SOMEONE

Stop putting everyone in front of you. What in the whole fuck?
YOU FIRST. Everyone else will be fine. Honestly, truly.

month:

TOP PRIORITIES / VITAL SHIT I MUST DO

- [ ] _____
- [ ] _____
- [ ] _____
- [ ] _____
- [ ] _____
- [ ] _____

IMPORTANT ASS DATES

BULLSHIT I SHOULD DO

- [ ] _____
- [ ] _____
- [ ] _____
- [ ] _____
- [ ] _____
- [ ] _____
- [ ] _____
- [ ] _____
- [ ] _____
- [ ] _____
- [ ] _____
- [ ] _____

SU	M	T	W	TH	F	S

WHERE THE FUCK IS MY MONEY GOING?

Personal Expense Tracker			
WRITE THAT SHIT DOWN!			
Date:	Description Of Expense:	Payment Type:	Amount:

ADD THAT SHIT UP: _____

WHERE THE FUCK IS MY MONEY GOING?

Personal Expense Tracker			
WRITE THAT SHIT DOWN!			
Date:	Description Of Expense:	Payment Type:	Amount:

ADD THAT SHIT UP: _____

ACCOMPLISHMENTS FOR THE MONTH, SUCK ASS FAILURES, GRATITUDE & OTHER

random shit

IMPORTANT SHIT I ACCOMPLISHED:

SHIT MY SORRY ASS DIDN'T GET DONE:

SHIT I WILL TRY HARDER TO DO NEXT MONTH(MAYBE):

A QUICK & EASY LIST OF SHIT I'M GRATEFUL FOR:

-
-
-

DOODLES & SHIT:

PEOPLE I WANT TO PUNCH:

-
-

OVERALL, THIS MONTH WAS:

O BASIC AS FUCK

O PRETTY AWESOME, ACTUALLY

O WHO CARES, I'M TIRED AF

O A SHIT SHOW, I PUNCHED SOMEONE

Life is tough, but not as tough as you.
Darling, life ain't got shit on you!

(lined note page)

bullshit notes

bullshit notes

bullshit notes

bullshit notes

bullshit notes

bullshit notes

bullshit notes

bullshit notes

bullshit notes

DOODLES & SHIT

DOODLES & SHIT

DOODLES & SHIT

DOODLES & SHIT

DOODLES & SHIT

DOODLES & SHIT

DOODLES & SHIT

DOODLES & SHIT

DOODLES & SHIT

DOODLES & SHIT

DOODLES & SHIT

Made in the USA
Coppell, TX
06 December 2024

41867462R00057